Me & My BIG Ideas

© 2014 Info Products (PTY) Ltd, All rights reserved.

No part of this publication may be reproduced or transmitted in any form or by any means, mechanical or electronic, including photocopying and recording, or by any information storage and retrieval system, without permission in writing from the authors (except by a reviewer, who may quote brief passages and/or show brief video clips in a review.)

Disclaimer: No portion of this material is intended to offer legal, medical, personal or financial advice. We've taken every effort to ensure we accurately represent these strategies and their potential to help you grow your business or your life. However, we do not purport this as a "get rich scheme" and there is no guarantee that you will earn any money using the content, strategies or techniques displayed here. Nothing in this presentation is a promise or guarantee of earnings. The content, case studies and examples shared in this book do not in any way represent the "average" or "typical" member experience. In fact, as with any product or service, we know that some members purchase our systems and never use them, and therefore get no results from their membership whatsoever. You should assume that you will obtain no results with this program. Therefore, the member case studies we are sharing can neither represent nor guarantee the current or future experience of other past, current or future members. Rather, these member case studies represent what is possible with our system. Each of these unique case studies, and any and all results reported in these case studies by individual members, are the culmination of numerous variable, many of which we cannot control, including pricing, target market conditions, product/service quality, offer, customer service, personal initiative, and countless other tangible and intangible factors. Your level of success in attaining similar results is dependent upon a number of factors including your skill, knowledge, ability, connections, dedication, business savvy, business focus, business goals, and financial situation. Because these factors differ according to individuals, we cannot guarantee your success, income level, or ability to earn revenue. You alone are responsible for your actions and results in life and business, and by your use of these materials, you agree not to attempt to hold us liable for any of your decisions, actions or results, at any time, under any circumstance. The information contained herein cannot replace or substitute for the services of trained professionals in any field, including, but not limited to, financial or legal matters.

Under no circumstances, including but not limited to negligence, will John Harris, Info Products (PTY) Ltd or any of its representatives or contractors be liable for any special or consequential damages that result from the use of, or the inability to use, the materials, information, or success strategies communicated through these materials, or any services following these materials, even if advised of the possibility of such damages.

Me & My BIG Ideas

ISBN: **978-1500780852** (paperback)

ISBN: **1500780855** (epub)

Published by:

Info Products (PTY) Ltd

17 Mimosa Street, Wilropark

Johannesburg, SA 1731

+2711 025 5462

www.expertindustry.co.za

Me & My BIG Ideas

Table of Contents		Page
About the Author		4
Introduction		5
Chapter 1	Mindset	7
Chapter 2	Old Economy	17
Chapter 3	New Economy	23
Chapter 4	Understanding Your Dreams	28
Chapter 5	Passion Driven Talents	39
Chapter 6	Taking Action	45
Chapter 7	Transform Yourself	55
Chapter 8	Make it Sustainable	62
Chapter 9	The Expert Industry	76

About the Author

John won the South African lightweight kickboxing championship in 1989. But found it was not his life's purpose. He loved traveling and started his own travel agency, which although extremely successful wasn't his true passion. Through extended travel market research he came across affiliate marketing, then social media marketing, which he also turned, into a successful company, this was in line with his passion but not the real deal. He felt that he had not fulfilled his God given purpose in life yet, there was still something missing. He came to the realization that his true purpose was to help other people reach their dreams. This led him into the wonderful world of information product creation.

He became the product creation expert and teaches small business owners, big corporations, entrepreneurs, authors, experts, speakers, coaches and consultants how to reach their dreams by turning their knowledge into income.

My passion is helping small business owners, big corporations, entrepreneurs, authors, experts, speakers, coaches and consultants reach their dreams by turning their knowledge into income.

Introduction

In today's volatile economy the threat of losing your job has become a very real possibility and consequently this has created a lot of fear in the general population. Even for those with a job the cost of living has become unaffordable.

I'm here to tell you that if you don't differentiate, break through the market clutter, capture imagination and attention and get prospects motivated about you, your idea or your business, you can and will become redundant.

Let's first talk about the opportunity, where the market and the money currently are.

Here's some data that should make you jump:

• The digital information market has more than doubled in the last 5 years... and every year:

- 33 billion dollars is spent in the corporate training and e-learning industry.
- 27.94 billion is spent in the eBook and book publishing industry
- 10.5 billion in the personal growth market
- 17 billion is spent in the mobile app market
- 1.2 billion is spent in the coaching market

But what does this mean to you?

It means in one word; OPPORTUNITY

You and I both know that we are in a down economy, but guess what the personal growth, information products, coaching and training industry is booming! THE NEW ECONOMY is growing.

Me & My BIG Ideas

It's an industry that grows in a down economy and it's in fact the best time to make the most money, because people are looking for solutions – for ways to improve their financial situation.

In a growing economy people take business and personal risks to grow. That means that now (in the down economy) is the time for you to bring your ideas to the marketplace and capitalize on what you know or maybe now is the right time to start making some good money from your existing products.

You have to do something different to change the results you are currently getting, and I truly hope that "Me & My BIG Ideas" gives you what you need to do something different.

Me & My BIG Ideas

Chapter 1

Mind-set

We believe that we cannot control our emotions. It is deemed an animate entity that comes to life unbidden. How then can you will yourself to feel? Can we manipulate our emotions?

Yes we can and we regularly do! By visiting a proverbial 'Happy Place' we aspire to peace and hope or joy when we are despondent. We actively lift our spirits by choosing to concentrate on pleasant things. The opposite however is true too. Our fortitude is tested and often strained when we try to bolster a friend in need of comfort, glee readily turns to gloom. In an effort to lend solace to another we often find ourselves drained of delight, disheartened by their distress.

Emotion is widely considered a combination of three components: perception, physical response and our expression of the aforementioned. Exploring these aspects allows us to control our reactions - recognising why we feel what we feel enables us to manage what we feel. It is essentially a frame of mind, changeable.

Psychologist Robert Plutchnik introduced a classification system called the "wheel of emotions" during the 80's. The 8 primary dimensions are: happiness vs. sadness; anger vs. fear; trust vs. disgust and surprise vs. anticipation. These key emotions combine in several ways. Fear and disgust might fuse and form contempt.

As such, emotion is rarely ever simple; a particular emotion cannot be explicitly defined.

It is however, the expression of emotion that we mainly relate to - by interpreting behaviour we are able to understand (or at least acknowledge) our own sentiments and those of others. Herein rests the clue.

Emotional intelligence, the capacity to correctly decipher demeanour, determines not only our relations with other but also decides how we contrive to exploit our feelings. Like a boxer "psyching" himself up before a fight - aggravating himself deliberately by enacting his body's instinctive physiological responses in an exaggerated fashion he mentally prepares himself for the task ahead.

Emotion can be an invaluable tool; anxiety about a looming exam will likely inspire you to ensure that you are well prepared; fear of failing will prompt you to study harder. Your emotional response to any given situation will prescribe your reaction. Adopting a composed disposition will generate equanimity and an improved sense of wellbeing. A calm tranquil manner is a choice, not easy but possible…

How exactly would I go about embracing serenity?

Get to know yourself, indulge in a session of honest and sincere introspection. Examine your thoughts… Uncover your very core and note what fires you up and what extinguishes the blaze. Strive for a healthy balance. List your talents and limitations. Formulate a sensible stratagem whereby you may nurture and encourage your skills whilst rendering the flaws without force.

Enlist the aid of a mentor, someone whom you trust to keep you inspired and focused – a comrade in arms to stand at your back when facing your inner demons shake your foundations, a champion to raise your arm in victory!

Accomplishing anything worthwhile takes time and effort. Overcoming customary patterns in favour of new, more constructive and elevating routines will require continuous hard work and commitment. If you practise these new habits consistently your life-changes will likely become usual and ordinary – a calm, balanced countenance will become commonplace.

We often abandon our efforts to soon. Weighing the desire to achieve against the pains required to attain our goals and promptly decide to quit. We lack ambition and drive.

For example, a young man may want to get a job as an electrician. Unfortunately the necessary qualifications are elaborate, involving arduous studies and a two-year apprenticeship. He considers this effort excessive and elects to work at McDonald's instead.

Perhaps he lacks confidence in his ability to complete the task as is frequently the case…

A girl wants to get into the school play. She dreams of having the lead role but before she attends the auditions she has already convinced herself that she isn't good enough thus she opts out.

Others are simply fickle! Wavering between alternatives they never bring a task to fruition, completing what they started. They falter due to uncertainty.

Determination breeds resolve. It is the fixed objective to overcome obstacles, like a student set on graduating from college despite financial hurdles or a baseball player intent on catching a ball seemingly out of reach. For as long as the possibility remains, a goal-orientated person will keep trying!

Determination is a blend of skill, knowledge and philosophy permitting the pursuit of ambition and aspiration, allowing for self-regulated, autonomous behaviour. A firm grasp of your aptitude coupled with conviction is essential. When acting on the basis of competence and attitude you have greater ability to take control of your life and assume the role of a successful individual.

Are you merely interested when it comes to getting paid to do what you love, or are you committed? Too many people stroll reflexively through life, tempted by a plethora of possibilities but not dedicated to making any of them a concrete truth.

What is the difference between interest and commitment?

- Interest reads a blog post; commitment applies that post day after day.
- Interest works an hour a day on your business; commitment works whenever time permits.
- Interest procrastinates; commitment focuses on what's important.
- Interest makes excuses; commitment constantly acquires new skills and solutions.

If you struggle with this issue, ask yourself:

Why are you holding back? What stops you from living the life you imagine for yourself?

Do you want it badly enough? If you persevere you will make it happen.

Me & My BIG Ideas

If the wearying thought of laboriously slaving away at an insignificant job in a dreary cubicle for the rest of your life is enough to rid you of apathy, I invite you to join me… and GO FOR IT!

You may be saying: "I *would* take action and get started, but I just don't know enough yet. I'm just not ready."

A pitiable pretext!

There is always more to learn. The amount of information on the internet is equivalent to a stack of books stretching from Earth to Pluto 10 times! If you keep waiting until you finish that book, podcast or video course, if you keep waiting until you are *ready,* you will never be ready.

You learn far more from experience than consumption. I learned more during my first product launch (1 week) than I did during the prior 6 months of ravenous information consumption. Concepts are introduced via information; *skills* are honed through action.

> "The best way to not feel hopeless is to get up and do something. Don't wait for good things to happen to you. If you go out and make some good things happen, you will fill the world with hope, you will fill yourself with hope."
> - Barack Obama

It was character that got us out of bed, commitment that moved us into action and discipline that enabled us to follow through.

Me & My BIG Ideas

Zig Ziglar

Accept your situation. It may seem counter-productive to accept your situation, but it gives rise to conception. It affords an opportunity in which to learn how to change the state of your affairs, what you need to avoid – it is *not* automatically resigning yourself to it. It is an admission of the origin of your anxiety. Realize that your situation is a healthy response to overwhelming stimuli, and that it can be dealt with in an equally healthy fashion.

Avoid your stress situations. Seems obvious, right? Sometimes staying away from bad situations is harder than it sounds. If you know a particular person or activity is the origin of your angst, simply cut it/them out of your life. If your condition is something more permanent i.e. work, school or family - find ways to spend time away from it. Taking time away from your circumstances is the first step towards relief.

Reframe your problems. Sometimes, a stressful scenario is just a matter of perspective. Instead of focusing on the problems that are causing you anxiety, concentrate on what is helpful. Revising your opinion can alter your stress-levels and your situation altogether. Do your best to see things in an optimistic light. Avoid cynicism at all costs.

Be better organized. Stress often arises from feeling overwhelmed. Use a planner to keep track of your "to do lists". Organization and prioritizing can help you break responsibilities down into manageable pieces and focus on the things that really matter to you. Staying on top of chores and errands will keep you in a positive mindset, and help you get more done in the long run.

When we are no longer able to change a situation - we are challenged to change ourselves.

Me & My BIG Ideas

Viktor E. Frankl

No one cares about your work-life balance more than you. On occasion I mentor young men and women who are concerned about the balance or lack thereof in their lives. I advise them that it is their responsibility to make sure their home and work life is equalized. You need to advocate yourself. Read your company policies and talk to your manager.

Family comes first, work second. I am always supportive when there is a personal situation that needs attention. However, I do not take their personal lives in consideration when I am delegating tasks or assigning projects. I rely on them to let me know if there is a conflict between the workload and their work-life balance. If your manager is not empowering you to speak up then you need to empower yourself. Early in my career it would never have occurred to me to talk to my staff about balancing their home and work life.

Prioritize what is important at work and at home. I am a people pleaser so I really do not like to say no to any request. What I have learned to say that has helped me tremendously is, "Yes, I can do that but this is where it sits on my list of priorities." Understanding the important things both at work and at home will help you concentrate your time on the tasks that matter the most.

Communicating the priority to the person making demands on your time also helps to set clear expectations for when they can expect the results. As we all know priorities can and do change so it is important to maintain that communication with the relevant party throughout the process. This feels more natural for me at work so let me give you an example for your home life.

Block time on the calendar for your home life, including time for yourself. At work I always know what I need to be doing because it is scheduled on my calendar. When I get home it is easy to be distracted and end up not accomplishing things that are important - especially spending quality time with your family and spending quality time alone. Blocking time out for these activities helps me align my family to the plan and ensures we take the time to connect with each other and ourselves.

> "True wealth, success, and happiness can only be achieved by balancing our business life with the duty we have to our self and to our family."
> - Joseph C. Kunz Jr.

Expect mistakes. Life's hard knocks are as common as life's success knocks. To expect the process of living to always be smooth sailing is to invite a lack of realism into your life. It happens to the best of us. Failure helps to create balance in your life and presents an opportunity for personal growth. Accepting the inevitability that things won't always go your way is an important part of avoiding becoming bitter and twisted, or of preventing yourself from simply resting on your laurels and never pushing further to realize your full potential.

- Learn to love finding out that you're wrong about something. That's not failure; it's enlightenment and the path to finding the right way.

Remind yourself that you are good enough. Not believing we are good enough rests at the heart of fearing failure. Failures serve as proof of this greatest fear, causing us to want to withdraw and not try again for fear of being further exposed as inadequate and incapable. However, this fear is not founded in reality; nobody is perfect and everyone will fail at various points in life. The real difference between people who become successful and overcome failure and those who do not comes down to how you manage failure and how you view its impact on you. Feeling inadequate is a commonplace human feeling that even very public, very successful people feel but they don't let it keep them down. You are good enough; all you need is to give yourself the go-ahead to keep trying.

Remain calm. Whatever you're feeling about a failure, don't lose your composure over it. Look at it this way – it won't make any difference to the outcome itself whether you blow your top or stay calm but it will take a lot less energy and maintain your reputation if you choose the latter response. If you're really frustrated and angry, channel these emotions to motivate you to start again.

- Don't take your anger out on others. It's not good to bottle up feelings, but you can't go around taking out your anger on those around you for any good reason. Go for a run, a swim, or a boxing session to relieve tension and give you space to think. Just do something focused and energized to distract you from the initial intense feelings until they calm.

Stop worrying, start laughing. Yes, the sun will come up again tomorrow. Yes, things might be miserable for a little while but how will worry help? Think back to a time when you worried a lot. Did it make any difference? Most likely not, apart from giving you more wrinkles and grey hair. The greatest thing you can do for yourself during failure is to inject humour into your reflection of what happened. While there will be a period in which you feel especially tender, being able to laugh at yourself for mistakes can be an important part of the healing process, readying you for moving on again. Being able to say "Oh I did that, ha, ha, such a way to stuff up, ha, ha!" is part of putting failure into perspective.

- Be very careful that you don't take on other people's mistakes or circumstances as being *your* failure. Humour is one way of telling you that you don't need to carry the world on your shoulders and that sometimes, things just happen, no matter what you do or do not do.

> "The greatest accomplishment is not in never falling, but in rising again after you fall."
>
> - Vince Lombardi

Chapter 2
The Old Economy

Trade is not a new occurrence - we've been bartering for centuries! Adam Smith illustrates barter as "higgling, haggling, swapping, dickering" or "selfish profiteering". It evolved considerably over time, became refined and now trade has come to include the complex dealings that transpire on the floor of the New York Stock Exchange (NYSE).

The basic elements of buying and selling in some form of a market however haven't changed a bit because ultimately, it involves giving one thing in exchange for another.

Trade is a basic economic concept that involves multiple parties participating in voluntary negotiations and the subsequent exchange of one's goods and/or services for the desired goods and/or services of another. The introduction of money as a medium of exchange allows trade to be conducted in a manner that is more systematic than the initial practice of bartering and so the erstwhile economy takes shape.

Bartering is an observable fact and every human being knows inherently how to haggle. It is an arrangement of exchange by which goods and/or services are directly exchanged for other goods and/or services without using money. It is distinct from gift economies in that the reciprocal exchange is immediate and not delayed in time. It is generally bilateral, but may be multilateral (i.e., mediated through barter organizations) and usually exists parallel to monetary systems in most developed countries though to a very limited extent. Barter generally replaces money as the method of exchange in times of monetary crisis - such as when the currency may be either unstable (e.g., hyperinflation or deflationary spiral) or simply unavailable for conducting commerce.

The barter system enables two parties to exchange goods or services based on a mutually perceived value.

To illustrate, a plumber can fix a baker's sink – a service for which the baker would normally have paid R100. Instead, the baker gives the plumber baked goods worth R100.

Another example would be a photographer agreeing to photograph a dentist's wedding pictures in return for some dental work of equal value.

These transactions do not involve any exchange of currency however each party benefits from the transaction.

But the question remains; does bartering have a place in a healthy economy? Its popularity fluctuates throughout history as national economies become either depressed or prosperous. In the 20th century we saw an increase in bartering during the U.S. depression of the 1930's as well as in post-World-War-II Europe and it becomes prevalent again during the extended recession of the early 1980's. When the economy is in good condition, people would rather spend their abundance of cash - but when inflation is high many people are unemployed and cash is less readily available, people want to bargain.

Bartering might however have found a permanent place in a healthy economy!

Me & My BIG Ideas

Commerce is the organization of an economy that constitutes an environment for business. The system includes the legal, economic, political, social, cultural and technological structures that are operational in any country. Thus commerce is an establishment or environment that affects the business prospects of an economy or a nation-state. It can also be defined as a component of business which includes all activities, functions and institutions involved in transferring goods from producers to consumers.

"Commerce is that part of business which is concerned with the exchange of goods and/or services and includes all those activities which directly or indirectly facilitate that exchange."

Human desires are never ending. It can be classified as *primary (fundamental)* - and *secondary needs*. Commerce has made distribution and movement of goods possible from one part of the world to the other. Today we can buy anything produced anywhere in the world. This in turn enabled man to satisfy his innumerable wants, thereby promoting social welfare.

The growth of commerce, industry and trade bring about the growth of agencies of trade for example banking, transport, warehousing and advertising agencies. These agencies need people to ensure its operation. Increase in production results in an increasing demand. Consequently, development of commerce generates more employment opportunities in a country which allows them to do financial transactions.

A financial transaction is an agreement, communication or movement carried out between a buyer and a seller in order to exchange an asset for payment. It involves a change in the status of the finances of two or more businesses or individuals. The buyer and seller are separate entities involved in the trade of items of value - information, goods, services and money.

It is still a transaction if the goods are exchanged at one time and the money at another. This is known as a two-part transaction: part one is giving the money; part two is receiving the goods.

In ancient times non-financial transactions were commonly conducted through methods of credit in which goods and/or services were exchanged for a promise of future recompense. Credit has certain disadvantages like necessitating those traders and their intermediaries trust one another or in the least rest assured that regulatory bodies exist to enforce agreements. Debts must eventually be settled with an accepted currency; services or a substance of value such as gold and silver.

Systems of credit are obvious throughout recorded history and from archaeology. Obsidian and flint was exchanged in the Stone Age, Lapis Lazuli in the Kassite period. During Greek civilization and the Roman Empire thereafter valuable spices were brought from the Far East to Europe. By contrast little evidence has been found of the widespread use of pure barter, when traders meet face to face and transactions are completed in a single swap.

Here are some examples of activities you might engage in daily that would be considered transactions:

- Buying or selling a stock

- Buying a cup of coffee

- Selling your freelance services

- Buying or selling a house

Deals were transacted in marketplaces or public markets; locations where vendors or merchants meet on a regular basis - a sponsoring entity has a legal and financial responsibility to oversee operations and at times provide facilities to house the market activity. A market typically assimilates traditional market activities such as the sale of fresh produce from open stalls and may also offer a wide range of different products - elements of specialized markets like farmers markets, craft markets and antique markets.

These markets formed the foundation of our economy but change is inevitable. Customarily public markets were owned and operated by city governments but this is no longer the case. Market places have fallen back into our own hands, the hand of the individual.

Why are these marketplaces not effective anymore?

The advent of the internet - the global village is also a global marketplace! The technological advances of the past few decades have given businesses the ability to grow and expand beyond local markets. E-commerce allows even small businesses to reach consumers worldwide, increasing their sales and profits. Unfortunately, along with the advantages come with disadvantages, creating challenges hitherto unknown.

Governments are investing millions of dollars in a New Economy, in 2014 during the World Economic Forum it was said that 'the New Economy is the way out of this financial crises we find ourselves in today'. If governments are trying to get away from the outmoded way of doing things, shouldn't you do the same?

———————

It is time to move your personal and professional life away from the dated way of doing things and realize that everything is changing whether you like it or not, you have to be part of the change or get left behind.

Me & My BIG Ideas

Chapter 3
The New Economy

Unless you are wholly ignorant you have likely heard the term robotics... But what exactly is robotics? How will robotics influence your future?

Robotics is the branch of technology that deals with the design, construction, operation and application of robots controlled with intricate computer systems which provide sensory feedback and aid in information processing. The robots are made to resemble humans in appearance and to mimic our behaviours and cognitive processes and are intended to replace us in dangerous situations and environments like defusing bombs and exploring shipwrecks. Today's robots are inspired by nature, contributing to bio-inspired robotics.

The concept of creating machines that can operate autonomously dates back to classical times but research into the functionality and potential uses of robots did not become significant until the 20th century. It now is a rapidly advancing technology – research and design combine to build new robots capable of serving a variety of practical purposes: domestic, commercial and military.

How will robotics influence your future? The New Economy is the driving force propelling automation! What would you give to spend more time with your family? Can you put a price on having more time to do what you love? Therein lies the future of robotics.

Me & My BIG Ideas

You attend to your passions whilst a robot handles your obligations. The New Economy has already had a huge impact on our lives via robotics even though for some it is a relatively new concept.

Artificial Intelligence (AI) is ingenuity demonstrated by machines or software. The study of Artificial Intelligence involves a number of sciences and professions including computer science, psychology, linguistics, philosophy and neuroscience as well as specialized fields such as artificial psychology. It's not only the manufacturing sector of the NME that will affect your life in the New Economy. The next component of the New Economy to contemplate is service. Would you be able to do more if you didn't actually need to be present?

A Service Economy refers to a financial concept which asserts that service is becoming increasingly more important in product management. While most manufacturing companies continue to sell tangible products, the service delivery that is being integrated into the product is becoming a market differentiator. The notion that products and services are interconnected and that service represents an increasingly important part of a product is called the servitization of products. *Servitization: The delivery of a service component as an added value when providing products.* The merging of products and service is said to take place on a service-product continuum.

Creating a saleable product is in itself a major feat but ensuring that the consumer understands the proper application thereof is an entirely different ball game. That is how products and services are linked. It doesn't really matter what you do in your business or in life, there will always be a group of people ahead of you and there will always be a band of people behind you. The latter assembly is the group you need to cater to; those are the people who will buy your products.

Suppose you're an author, coach, speaker, consultant, entrepreneur, small business owner or expert - what would it mean to the collection of people behind you if you rendered a service to them enabling them to get to where you currently are? Would you be prepared to pay to get where to the same level as the crowd ahead of you? By offering services as an added value to your primary product you will cement your future in a service-based economy.

Not only is a comprehensive knowledge of the New Economy vital in order for you to prosper. It is an economy on its own!

So how can one become a part of the knowledge economy?

Firstly we have to understand that your knowledge and experiences are unique. Every living creature on this planet has unique experiences, knowledge and expertise. Some of us may have experience in the same field but it will not be the same – what happens to some does not happen to everyone.

The knowledge economy is also known as the expert industry but what qualifies you as a specialist? An expert is someone widely recognized as a reliable source of technique or skill whose faculty for judging or deciding rightly; justly or wisely is accorded authority and status by their peers or the public in a specific distinguished domain.

An expert, more generally, is a person with extensive knowledge or ability based on research, experience or occupation in a particular area of study. Professionals are called in for advice on their respective subjects but they do not always agree on the particulars of a field of study. An expert can be, by virtue of credential, training, education, profession, publication or experience, believed to have special knowledge of a subject beyond that of the average person, sufficient that others may officially (and legally) rely upon the individual's opinion.

It stands to reason then that you already are the authority to the group of people currently following behind you - they will value your expert opinion!

You are a cog in the clock which is the New Economy. You must cease every viable opportunity available to set the system to your advantage. The New Economy is emerging at the speed of light but what is prompting its growth? Who or what allowed this new phenomenon to develop at an exponential pace? Information is the key – the ability to share information with each other allowed humanity to consistently overcome and conquer all the hurdles pitted against us. Knowledge is the gateway to attaining your dreams. You have to be prepared to identify, improvise, implement and prioritize in all aspects of life; you have to be part of the informational revolution!

'The informational revolution is not an apple that falls when it is ripe. You have to make it fall'.

The Information Age (also known as the Computer Age, Digital Age or New Media Age) is a period in human history characterized by the shift from traditional industry that the industrial revolution brought through industrialization, to an economy based on information computerization. The onset of the Information Age is associated with the Digital Revolution, just as the Industrial Revolution marked the onset of the Industrial Age.

During the information age, the phenomenon is that the digital industry creates a knowledge-based society surrounded by a high-tech global economy that spans over its influence on how the manufacturing throughput and the service sector operate in an efficient and convenient way. In a commercialized society, the information industry is able to allow individuals to explore their personalized needs, therefore simplifying the procedure of making decisions for transactions and significantly lowering costs for both the producers and buyers.

This presents you with profitable prospects! Amidst the opportunities in the Information Age revolution is the how-to industry. You can effectively earn revenue by teaching your abilities to those who may benefit from it, in essence doubling your income by simply doing what you need to anyway.

> "Change will not come if we wait for some other person or some other time. We are the ones we've been waiting for. We are the change that we seek."
>
> - Barack Obama

Chapter 4

Understanding your Dreams

Dreaming is a communication of the body, mind and spirit in a symbolic unrestrained state, a link between our conscious mind and our unconscious mind helping to create wholeness, "Dreams are the bridge that allows movement back and forth between what we think we know and what we really know". It is the process in which your mind orders the confusion of data contained within your long - and short term memory.

To correctly interpret your dreams you have to understand what dreams are – in essence it is a succession of images, ideas, emotions, and sensations that emerge as a visual screenplay spontaneously during certain cycles of sleep.

Dreams chiefly happen when you enter a state of brain wave activity akin to that of being awake – REM or Rapid Eye Movement. As the name suggests REM sleep is identified by continuous movements of the eyes whilst asleep. At times, dreams do occur during other stages of sleep however these dreams tend to be much less vivid or memorable. The length of a dream varies; it may last for a mere few seconds or as long as 30 minutes. On average a person has three to five dreams per night but sometimes you may have up to seven dreams in one night and as the night progresses your dreams tend to last longer.

Me & My BIG Ideas

"Dreams also allow us to process information or events that may be painful or confusing in an environment that is at once emotionally real but physically unreal". Dreaming permits us to act out painful or puzzling emotions or experiences in a safe place. It is a remarkable tool with which to face difficulties head-on!

Your dreams reveal your innermost desires and your secret wounds thus analysing your dreams can help you gain a sensible and practical understanding of yourself.

When examining your dreams there is no set of stringent rules people need to follow, no method to observe. Every person is unique so there are no formulas or prescriptions! Dreams *"can only be understood in the larger context of the individual's unfolding and self-discovery, however, there are several guidelines that can help you see your dreams more thoughtfully and dig deeper into their meaning.*

Remember you're the expert. *"There are no experts other than you when it comes to your own psyche so don't stop trusting your own inner guide to your unconscious."*

Therapists need to place aside all of their information, tools and associations for universal symbols and dream interpretation with each new client and treat each person as a unique, new world to be discovered."

Identify how you were feeling in the dream. For example, ask yourself: "Was I scared, angry, remorseful, etc.? Do I still feel those feelings the morning after? How comfortable am I feeling these feelings?" The more comfortable you feel about the feelings you feel the closer you will come to discovering your destiny and live the life that you are meant to live.

Me & My BIG Ideas

"The better you can remember your dreams, the better you will be able to analyse and follow them"

Everyone dreams; some cultures believe that everything dreams including animals, rivers, trees and the earth itself. Not remembering dreams is common. Sometimes this happens because people "live" in "normal" reality so much that their consciousness disavows dreams and dreaming; sometimes because the day-to-day is so full that no space or place is made to hang out with the night's dream. Before you go to sleep ask yourself, the spirit, your pillow, your stuffed animals or whomever you pray to, "Tonight, help me remember my dreams." This helps build a friendly atmosphere, a kind of welcoming to your dreams, the dream world, or the "dream-maker." Further, take more time waking up, slow down, stay open and dreamy a little longer—your dreams may sense your invitation and reward you with an image, a feeling, a smell or a memory.

Even if you remember only the smallest snippet, write it down, record it (More about this in a moment). Dreams are holographic—that means that each fragment of a dream is connected to the whole. If you "pull" on that clip, like pulling a thread, the whole dream and its meaning will unfold and reveal itself.

This brings us to the most vital part in understanding your dreams - recording your dreams!

It is the first and most important step in analysing your dream. "Taking notes, even a few sentences that encapsulate the dream, literally draws the content of the unconscious out into the realm of the concrete."

Think you don't dream or can't remember your dreams? Simply keep a journal by your bed, and write it down "No dream to record" every morning. "Within two weeks of this process, the person will begin to remember their dreams." (In fact, "you might open the floodgates!")

Calm your mind and body before bedtime. Is your brain typically buzzing before bed? Having a lot of stressful thoughts in your head can make it harder to remember your dreams, which requires deep focus. Before you go to bed, let your mind relax and be free of heavy thoughts. Drift calmly into sleep.

Think about a major problem or emotional concern right before you fall asleep. Think deeply about the situation without pressing for solutions or coming to conclusions. Just thinking about the problem opens the door, in a sense, to more vividly remembered dreams, and the dreams may in turn offer more insights regarding the problem at hand.

Concentrate on recalling your dream as soon as you wake up. Typically you can remember only the last dream you had before waking. Don't move or do anything. Stay in the same position as the one in which you awoke and try to remember as much about your dream as possible before you think about anything else. Think it through from start to finish. Once you have a clear memory of what you dreamt about write it down.

It's important to figure out what your dreams are telling you. They are intuition — the part of ourselves that knows what's best, they warn us and they inspire us; they let us know when we are going off track. So never dismiss them by saying "it's only a dream." It contains the answers you need right now for your life.

But dreams don't always tell a simple story and the field of dream research becomes even more fascinating when people from different cultures and backgrounds report having similar dreams.

Me & My BIG Ideas

Here are some meanings of dreams that helped others just like you understand their dreams but as I said before, "There are no experts other than you when it comes to your own psyche, so don't stop trusting your own inner guide to your unconscious".

Alphabet

Dreaming about the letters of the alphabet can symbolize an object, animal or a place associated with or resembling that particular letter. A letter can also trigger your memory of a person. Alternatively the alphabet refers to the primitive stages of understanding some concept or emotion.

Animals

Seeing animals in your dream points to your instinctual needs and desires that may be repressed in your waking life. Each animal has specific characteristics that will help guide you as to what your subconscious is trying to reveal.

Birds

Seeing birds in your dream symbolize your goals, aspirations and hopes. They also reflect joy, harmony, ecstasy, balance and love. You are experiencing spiritual freedom and psychological liberation. The significance of specific birds in dreams is based on their colour, behaviour and the sounds they make. These qualities help pinpoint a more meaningful interpretation of your dream.

Body Parts

Your dream body represents your dream ego and your conscious identity. In many ancient cultures the body was seen as a metaphor for the spiritual world. Specific body parts are especially significant if they are abnormal or different. In some cases, your dream may forewarn of health problems and concerns regarding that particular body part.

Bugs

What's "bugging" you? Dreaming of bugs and insects suggest that you are worried about something. They are symbolic of your anxieties and fears. Also consider the popular phrase "bitten by the bug" to imply your strong emotional ties or obsession with some activity, interest or hobby. On the other hand a bug may be representative of your sexual thoughts. The various bugs or insects in your dream help clue you in as to what may be troubling you.

Cars

Your dream car is indicative of your drive and ambition. What happens with your dream car reflects your ability to navigate from one stage of your life to another. Where you go in your dream car symbolizes your goals and dreaming about specific parts of your car provides clues about your status and your ability to achieve those goals.

Characters

An important concept to keep in mind about the characters you see or the characters you become in your dream is to first mull over how they represent an aspect of your own self. The dream characters may appear in your dream to call attention to certain qualities that you are lacking. They can depict or exaggerate certain qualities as a way of focusing your attention on them. Some people in your dream can also represent your unfinished communication with them and they may continue to appear in your dream until the conflict is resolved.

Me & My BIG Ideas

Clothing

How you are perceived or the act you may be putting on in front of others can be reflected in the types of clothes you have on in your dream. Clothing in dreams also signifies your condition or status in an area of your waking life.

Colours

Colours are very subjective and personal therefore first consider your own personal associations with the colour in your dream. Does it remind you of a particular person, a body part, a childhood toy, some object, etc? For example, the colour yellow may remind you of the childhood school bus you rode in but for someone else it may remind them of the yellow house they grew up in. Colours in dreams can also convey emotions.

Common

What symbols are Dream Aficionados' looking up and emailing in about the most? These are the Top 20 Most Common Symbols being dreamt according to popular observation.

Death

Dreams about death can be alarming regardless who dies, whether it is you or a loved one. Dreaming of death is usually more symbolic and often indicates an ending of a particular habit, behaviour, circumstance etc. More directly, dreaming about death can be part of the grieving process if you recently experienced the passing of a loved one.

Disasters

The fear of not knowing what is in your future can be the reason why you are having a disaster dream. Specific disasters point to the area of your waking life in which you are experiencing anxiety, doubt or lack of control.

Feelings

The emotions in your dream are usually never disguised. This means that the feelings you experience in your dreams are not symbolic of something else but rather reflections of your true, honest feelings. Such feelings may have been suppressed during the day and are being expressed in your dreams when your defences are down. Feelings expressed in dreams can help you deal with depression, guilt and other complex emotions.

Negative emotions tend to occur twice as often as pleasant feelings. Fear and anxiety are the most commonly expressed emotions in dreams followed by anger and sadness.

Food

Food for thought? Dreaming about food refers to thoughts, ideas and beliefs. They are trying to convey an idea that you need to take in and digest mentally.

House

Your dream house is symbolic of the Self, while the rooms inside the house relate to various aspects of your identity and to the many facets of your personality. The attic refers to the mind, while the basement represents the subconscious.

Numbers

To see certain numbers in your dream provide encouragement or discouragement. Numbers reflect how or where you stand in some area of your waking life. Sometimes numbers may not appear directly and can be presented in the number of characters, number of objects or an action that is repeated a certain number of times.

Also worth noting is that odd numbers are considered more aggressive then even numbers, while even numbers are considered to be more tranquil.

In general, you want to stick with the basic numbers (1 through 9) when trying to decipher the meaning of multiple digit numbers. For example, the number "1965" could mean the year 1965. But you can also add up the digits until you get a single digit number. Thus 1965 --> 1+9+6+5 = 21 --> 2+1 = 3.

Places

When trying to decipher the significance of your dream place or surrounding, pay attention to the look and feel of the landscape. If it is a place you have never been to or seen, ask yourself if you have been anywhere which brings about similar feelings or if it reminds you of another place and time in your life. Sometimes the places in your dream may also represent an idea or a person.

Pregnancy

Pregnancy dreams symbolize an aspect of yourself or your life that is growing and developing. Being pregnant in your dream may also represent the birth of a new idea, direction, project or goal. For those who are actually pregnant the dreams are more about the anxieties pertaining to the pregnancy.

Relationships

She loves me, she loves me not. Relationships can be difficult as is but then you have a dream… it can drive you crazy! Your dream relationship usually parallels your waking relationship in some way and may be highlighting something that is wrong in the relationship. In your dream state you are more inclined to confront issues that you would normally ignore or are afraid of bringing up. Compare your dream relationship with your waking relationship.

School

Dreaming about school, points to feelings of inadequacy and angst about your ability. If you are no longer in school such dreams may point to unresolved childhood issues. The dream may also reflect a life lesson that you need to learn.

Sex

Let's talk about sex! Sex dreams are about the merging of contrasting aspects about yourself. You need to incorporate certain qualities into your own character. The specific sex act parallels characteristics of yourself that you want to express. More directly, sex dreams are about sex and your desire for a physical connection.

Tools

The tools you see or use in your dream are about self-expression. They serve to highlight your skills and abilities. On the other hand, tools can also refer to some aspect of your waking life that needs to be fixed or needs your attention.

Travel

Travel dreams represent the path toward your life goals. Travelling to specific destinations often has a straightforward meaning of wanting to escape from your daily burden.

Me & My BIG Ideas

Vanity

Mirror, mirror on the wall who is the fairest of them all? Dreams about your looks are almost always about the persona you portray to others and how you want others to view you. These dreams also reflect insecurities and low self-esteem.

Wedding

Wedding dream symbolism is about new beginnings, changes and transitions. Not all wedding dreams are positive and can also reflect bitterness, sorrow, fear or even death. More directly, the stress of planning a wedding can often bring about dreams about your wedding.

Me & My BIG Ideas

Chapter 5

Passion Driven Talents

Discover your passion and you are bound for prosperity! Passion is an emotion as distinguished from reason; an intense, driving or overmastering feeling or conviction – an intense emotion compelling action... Your passion is your driving force! Fervour can coerce you into pursuing your goals.

People are motivated for different reasons i.e. a passion for your chosen profession. When you are zealous about your career you will likely be less mindful of principles and more vigilant about your performance, resulting in greater successes and heightened levels of psychological well-being. Enthusiasm for your job persuades you to go the extra mile helping you to realize your aspirations. Conversely when you are unfulfilled at work as in any one facet of your life the misery leaks throughout the whole, infecting your relationships and introducing psychological distress. Unless you act on your own ambition you will always tender lacklustre effort at best – slogging away at someone else's dreams is a recipe for failure.

A firm commitment to your vocation may however strain your personal relationships thus observing a balance is vital. Not only do we juggle relationships, we cannot deny the myriad of further interests... Several pursuits clamour for your attention and in an age of immediate gratification we want everything now! Symmetry is thus imperative.

Me & My BIG Ideas

Coaches encourage their personal development students to record their goals and list it in sequence according to priorities. Allot your time and energy appropriately. The amount of each invested in the respective activities ought to correspond with said activity's significance - if your family is on the top of your list you will surely spend more time with your family than on the pottery project which is at the bottom of your list.

Once you have identified your passions and sorted them in order of import, you have to isolate the relevant talents and skills. If you find yourself lacking, you have ample reason to better yourself – to acquire the necessary expertise. Your passion is your motivation!

How can you improve your proficiency?

Talent translates as the skill that someone has naturally to do something that is demanding. A talented person is effortlessly adept. It is an innate competence - a high degree of ability or of aptitudes. Despite being 'born with talent' we still have to work hard at evolving it. Practice makes perfect! In fact, an inborn flair is not essential. Some people become quite good at something even if they do not have much talent, hard work is often the deciding factor.

> **"You have talent; the people you see every day have talent! Find your talents, use it, and make it sustainable!"**

Learning something new can be daunting! The following 5 steps will augment your education allowing for maximum results. Apply these steps to anything you wish to study.

1. **Avoid feeling anxious.** The most common barrier to learning efficiently is anxiety. When we tell ourselves that something is hard and that we are not clever enough/able enough to learn it, it becomes a self-fulfilling prophecy and we become anxious. Anxiety

causes our thinking processes to slow down and we react with our emotions and desire to run or hide, rather than sitting down to calmly think through the task at hand. If you feel panicked, anxious, short of breath, scared, etc., when learning something new, look at dealing with your anxiety first.

2. **Break down the information and tasks into small lots.** Don't try to revise all of the information at once as that will only overwhelm you and cause you to feel that it's too difficult. Good approaches instead include:

- ✓ Reading the information slowly and taking regular breaks – come back to it frequently in between doing other activities (this allows your mind a rest but it's still digesting the information).
- ✓ Taking notes, making diagrams, using colour-coding or highlighting, reading out loud, repeating concepts and mini self-tests are all ways that might help you depending on what you are learning.
- ✓ Attempt the instruction over a period of time rather than in one single moment. Your mind cannot absorb everything at once but is much more adroit at gradual intake; if you have a week to learn it, take the whole week; don't leave it to the night before class or a presentation (see anxiety above!)
- ✓ Read the information, period. Sometimes we're afflicted with a lack of willingness to read the new information provided to us and hope we can wing it. There is only so much quick learning you will ever get out of "winging it". Persevere and read it.

3. **Find your learning style.** There are many different learning styles based on your personal strengths. Some people are more reliant on visual comprehension, others on aural comprehension and still

others need tactile sensations. Many of us are a combination of learning styles and it is only through trial and error that we find out what works for us. Once you have identified your preferred learning style rely on that to help you make sense of new information. If that means taking a complex university level textbook and drawing images of the concepts in a comic strip then by all means do it! You'll be one ahead of the person who hasn't a clue how to make that information stick...

4. **Ask questions.** This is absolutely the key to quick learning. As soon as those questions pop into your head, listen to them! They are there because your mind is attempting to get across the complexity of the new information before you and this is one means of breaking down the information into digestible pieces. And remember, even if the instructor is of the "ask no stupid questions" type, there is no such thing as a stupid question.

5. **Review your mistakes and the suggestions and comments from those tutoring you.** Nothing aids quick learning more than being in the position to reflect over where we have erred in the learning process. The lessons from this exercise often last the longest and are the fastest to take in.

How much easier would it be to learn a new skill if you are avidly interested in it? That's why you need to find a connection between your passions and talents. When you find this connection, your talents or skills are driven by your passion.

> *"Finding a connection between your passions and talents means that you will never have to work another day in your life"*

Work will become play!

Me & My BIG Ideas

Reconsider your strengths, talents and passions regularly so that you can maintain a level self-awareness. Why? Because things change and that's OK! As they change you can adapt, adjust course and remain inspired. Tapping into your strengths, talents and passions helps you to manage your day- to-day working life and longer-term career decisions in order to do the things you really want to do in life. It sharpens your edge in all areas.

"If you cannot find a connection between your passions and talents, try and obtain outside feedback"

Every so often ask people you respect for their criticism. Select individuals you know to be knowledgeable, someone who will be candid but fair-minded. Remember that another's opinions are subject to their experiences and thus imperfect and biased so don't take any one opinion as gospel. Well-intentioned advice can be insincere - they may just want to make you feel good, perhaps they are uncomfortable telling you the truth. The estimations of outsiders can be very helpful! It might help you discover a talent or skill you didn't realise you had.

Uncover your passion driven talents and make it sustainable!

How do you turn your passions and talents into income?

Once again we shift our attention to "that group of people" behind us.

If you are eager to invest to enrich yourself or become a number one investor like Warren Buffet; what would you gain if you could learn investment from Warren Buffet? In this example you are in that "group of people" behind him - he has products and courses to instruct you.

Me & My BIG Ideas

The same applies to you and those following in your footsteps... Those behind you are currently at a roadblock in their progress and they will pay you to help them overcome that roadblock. You can be the Warren Buffet of your industry!

Chapter 6
Taking Action

8 Ways to grow the action habit!

Now is your moment, right now - this instant! The words you're reading right here on this page mark each and every second of your precious life floating past.

Take action now to find your true purpose in life. Discover what it is that will fill you with delight. Live every second of your life! You deserve the joy of living.

Get yourself into a boat, take the paddle and row with the current to where you want to be, where you want to go, where you know you will find happiness and fulfilment.

Don't wait until next year or when the time feels right... Think about what it is you want in life and where you want to be and take the first step into that future.

The time is now. Take action right now!

Conditions

If you are waiting for conditions to be perfect before you start, you probably never will. There will always be something that isn't quite right. The timing is off, the market is down or there is just too much competition. In the real world there is no perfect time to start. You have to take action and deal with problems as they arise. The best time to start was last year. The second best time is right now.

Ask yourself these questions:

1. Do I want to increase my income (grow my business)?

2. Do I want to develop myself?

3. Do I want to grow my client base?

4. Do I want to create more free time?

If you answered yes to at least one of those questions then taking action now is the best thing you can do for you and your business. Just for a moment, let's go back to the reason(s) you became an entrepreneur. There may be many reasons but they are all probably related to the following benefits:

- More free time

- Work from home

- Freedom to make money doing what you enjoy

- Independence, flexibility, freedom with schedule

- Unlimited earning potential

- Didn't want to work for anyone

Let's take a look at some of the benefits of taking action now.

1. Increase Revenue

This should always be the first priority with your business. When you increase sales, you increase income and that creates more leverage. The more leverage you have the easier it is to create a business that fits your lifestyle. Taking action is pivotal to increasing sales so do not delay, do not wait... Take action now. Whatever ideas you have to increase revenue, implement that new service or product and get the word out.

2. Attract New Clients

When you create or enhance new products and/or services, you have the opportunity to attract new clients. It's important to add or enhance at least one product or service each year to keep the business fresh and in view of your clients. Use the launch of a product or service to gain "buzz" by sending an email to existing clients. Offer a "loyalty" discount to existing clients and their friends. You should also post the product or service on your website; link your social networking accounts (LinkedIn, Facebook, etc.) to that page and offer a "pre-launch" discount.

3. Enhance Company Brand and Reputation

Which businesses most frequently come to the mind of consumers? Businesses that consistently demand attention come to mind most often. Clients must be able to see and hear you. Keep the "buzz" going whether it's by an email campaign; follow up phone calls, special announcements, mailers or advertising, etc. Being an "expert" is not the most important factor, the key is taking action. The only thing you need to concern yourself with is delivering the results that you say you can deliver. When clients need help they will come to you because you are in the forefront of their minds. That in itself conveys the perception of a company with a well-respected brand and reputation.

Every time you take action, you take a step ahead of the competition. As an entrepreneur you are well aware that there are other businesses offering the same product or service you do. So, how do you stand out in a crowd? Make yourself heard! When you have an idea, take action. It takes a single idea to catapult your success but it takes consistent action to stay ahead of the competition. Getting ready to get ready or waiting until something is perfect does not serve you well. Stop getting ready to get ready and jump in.

"Don't wait until conditions are perfect – If you're waiting to start until conditions are perfect, you probably never will, be a doer, you'll get more done and stimulate new ideas in the process"

Be a Doer

Henry Ford was known to say: "You don't build a reputation on what you are going to do." Of course it's not just about reputation. By striving to be more productive the rewards are personal satisfaction, more exciting days, possibly more income and much more besides. Reputation is simply a side product of a successful life.

We all have dreams. We all have plans, ideas, goals and aspirations. The difficult bit is turning them into reality but all journeys begin with a single step and it's this step that turns out to be the most important. Turning something you want to do into something you are doing is the difference between possible success and certain failure.

Talk is cheap. Actions speak louder than words - this should be your mantra. Nobody is going to buy something that you plan to do (unless perhaps you're established at something, but even then you will always be expected to deliver). Nobody's lives are improved by something that you're thinking of doing.

In becoming a doer you transform yourself (which we will discuss in chapter 7) from being an observer into someone who is actually living in the thick of it. You will stand above everyone who is still talking about what they plan to do.

The best way to become a doer is to simply make a start. Starting a task will break it free from limbo and once in progress you will find it much easier to continue. Momentum will build and the task will be well underway. Make that start and you will have taken the hardest step.

Ideas alone don't bring success

Ideas are important but they are only valuable after they've been implemented. One average idea that's been put into action is more valuable than a dozen brilliant ideas that you are saving for "some other day" or the "right opportunity". If you have an idea that you really believe in, do something about it! Unless you take action it will never go anywhere.

You can't take action until you believe in yourself enough to handle the consequences of your decisions. Any time you assume the responsibility to give something that had not existed before an opportunity to become a reality – you become accountable for your actions.

Accountability requires believing in yourself enough to be 100% dedicated to getting the work done. Most people fail to take an idea to fruition because the unexpected challenges become more than they think they can handle and they no longer want to be accountable. They lose faith in themselves to see things through all the way to the end.

Never grow complacent. You can always expand upon your idea and make it better. When you begin to see how the dots connect, challenge yourself and your personal board of advisors to make your ideas even better.

This is what Steve Jobs did with Apple, Pixar Animation and Apple again. Continuous improvements were part of his legacy. He never stopped thinking of ways to upgrade his ideas. The Japanese have a name for it: Kaizen.

Use action to overcome fear

Have you ever noticed that the most difficult part of public speaking is waiting for your turn to speak? Even professional speakers and actors experience pre-performance anxiety. Once they get started the fear disappears. Action is the best cure for fear. The most difficult time to take action is the very first time. After the ball is rolling you'll build confidence and things will keep getting easier. Kill fear by taking action and build on that confidence.

No matter how overwhelming the situation, the best thing you can do is to take the next step. Pick an action that will move you forward, even if it's a small step and do it. The worst thing to do when things become intense is to stop. When you stop you make room for doubts and fears to taint your thinking and the more of this destructive force that you allow into your mind, the harder it is to get moving again.

The next time you feel yourself getting sucked into the vortex, take the next step on your journey. Doing anything that moves you forward will break you free from feelings of fear and doubt. Action restores faith and gives you energy.

> *"Action cures fear, become a doer and never be afraid of anything again"*

Me & My BIG Ideas

Start your creative "engine" automatically

One of the biggest misconceptions about creative work is that it can only be done when inspiration strikes. If you wait for inspiration to slap you in the face your work sessions will be few and far between. Instead of waiting, start your creative motor automatically. If you need to write something, force yourself to sit down and write. Put pen to paper. Brainstorm. Doodle... By moving your hands you'll stimulate the flow of ideas and inspire yourself.

Creativity leads to affluence - how do you boost your creativity?

Commit Yourself to Developing Your Creativity. The first step is to fully devote yourself to developing your creative abilities. Do not dally! Set goals, enlist the help of others and put time aside each day to develop your skills.

Become an Expert. One of the best ways to develop creativity is to become an expert in that area. By having a rich understanding of the topic you will be better able to think of novel or innovative solutions to problems.

Be willing to take risks. When it comes to building your creative skills you need to be willing to take risks in order to advance your abilities. While your efforts may not lead to success every time you will still be boosting your creative talents and building skills that will serve you well in the future.

Fight Your Fear of Failure. The fear that you might make a mistake or fail in your efforts can paralyze your progress. Whenever you find yourself harbouring such feelings, remind yourself that mistakes are simply part of the process. While you may occasionally stumble on your path to creativity you will eventually reach your goals.

Brainstorm to Inspire New Ideas. Brainstorming is a common technique in both academic and professional settings but it can also be a powerful tool for developing your creativity. Start by suspending your judgment and self-criticism then start writing down related ideas and possible solutions. The goal is to generate as many ideas as possible in a relatively short span of time. Next, focus on clarifying and refining your ideas in order to arrive at the best possible choice.

Live in the present

What does it mean to live fully in the present? It means that your awareness is completely centred on the here and now. You are not worrying about the future or reminiscing about the past. When you live in the present you live where life is happening. The past and future are illusions, they don't exist. As the saying goes "tomorrow never comes". Tomorrow is only a concept, tomorrow is always waiting to come around the corner but around that corner you'll find only vague shadows because time is always right now.

Why living in the present will change your life. If you're not living in the present you are living a sham - that seems to be a pretty good reason to live in the present, doesn't it? But how often are we worrying about things that haven't yet happened? How often do we chastise ourselves for mistakes we've made no matter how much time has passed? The answer is too often. Not only will living in the present have a dramatic effect on your emotional well-being, it can also impact your physical health. It's long been known that the amount of mental stress you carry can have a detrimental effect on your health. If you're living in the present, you're living in acceptance. You're accepting life as it is now, not as how you wish it would have been. When you're living in acceptance you realize everything is complete as it is. You can forgive yourself for the mistakes you've made and you can have peace in your heart knowing that everything that should happen will.

Focus on what you can do in the present moment. Don't worry about what you should have done last week or what you might be able to do tomorrow. The only time you can affect is the present. If you speculate too much about the past or the future you won't get anything done. Tomorrow or next week frequently turns into never.

Get down to business immediately

It's common practice for people to socialize and make small talk at the beginning of meetings. The same is true for individual workers. How often do you check email or RSS feeds before doing any real work? These distractions will cost you a lot of time if you don't bypass them and get down to business immediately. By becoming someone who gets to the point you'll be more productive and people will look to you as a leader.

It takes courage to take action without instructions from the person in charge. Perhaps that's why initiative is a rare quality that's coveted by managers and executives everywhere. Seize the initiative. When you have a good idea, start implementing it without being told. Once people see you're serious about getting things done they'll want to join in. The people at the top don't have anyone telling them what to do. If you want to join them, you should get used to acting independently.

Start Small

How many times have we told ourselves in complete earnestness, "I'm going to be more organized and productive from now on."? Or that the diet starts tomorrow? Or that we're going to make a real effort to exercise now?

Me & My BIG Ideas

Only to have that enthusiasm fizzle away and all our best intentions come to nothing?

So how do we start small?

Get moving a bit at a time. Inertia is beat only by movement. Once you get going momentum builds up and indolence is no longer a factor. So the key is to get started, not by trying to go from 0 to 60 in 5 seconds but by trying to go from 0 to 5mph in a day or two. That's doable. It's all about baby steps. Once you get going, you're golden.

Make a date, right now. Good intentions mean nothing if you don't actually get started and the only way to get started is to take action, right now - not tomorrow, not later today, not in an hour, not when you finish reading this chapter - right now! Look at your calendar, and make an appointment to create your action plan or to take the first action ("Go walking at 5:30 p.m. today in the park," for example). What's the first action you can take to make your desires a reality? Create a healthier meal plan for tomorrow? Arrange a place for everything you use at work so that your organizing system doesn't fall apart in two days? Decide what your first action will be and make an appointment for it, right now. Second part of this step: make that appointment the most important appointment on your schedule, more important than a doctor's appointment or a meeting with your boss. Set a small, achievable goal and take baby steps towards it.

Me & My BIG Ideas

Chapter 7

Transform Yourself

Successful people have one thing in common: they focus on strengths and manage weaknesses. You live in a noisy world with demands and expectations from all kinds of well-intentioned people that can pull you in the wrong direction. To make the most of your talents and abilities, you have to learn how to turn up the "Signal to Noise" ratio in favour of your strengths.

Strengths are not just what you're good and weaknesses are not simply what you're bad at.

We've all be raised to believe that our strengths are best judged by the success we achieve. If that's the case, then strength is the same as performance but we instinctively know that's not true. If you're like most people, you have some activities or tasks you do well, but hate doing. You have the ability; you can do it. You just wish you never had to do it again because it drains you. Such activities cannot be called strengths. They are weaknesses.

The simplest and best definition of strength is "an activity that strengthens you." And the proper definition of a weakness is "an activity that weakens you" - even if you're good at it.

Take responsibility for claiming your strengths by recognizing the signs. A strength is an activity that strengthens you but it can be hard to pay attention in the course of a busy workday to how what we do makes us feel. Train yourself to notice the SIGNs of strength:

• **S**uccess — when you do the activity, you feel effective and in control (what psychologists call "self-efficacy").

• **I**nstinct — before you do the activity, you look forward to doing it. You can't wait to do it!

• **G**rowth — while you are doing the activity, you feel inquisitive and focused. You may lose track of time and two hours feel like only five minutes have passed.

• **N**eeds — after you've done the activity, even if you're tired, you feel fulfilled. You can't turn a weakness into a strength, but you can take steps to stop or minimize the impact a weakness is having on you.

STOP doing it and see whether anybody notices. This won't work all or even most of the time, but sometimes a process or a task has become redundant and won't be missed.

 Team Up with someone who is strengthened by what weakens you. For every person drained or bored by an activity, there is someone — believe it or not — who finds the same task invigorating.

Offer up a strength so deliberately, so insistently, that doing it becomes valuable enough to take up more and more of your time, crowding out time spent on weaknesses. Take the best of your job and turn it into the most of your job.

Perceive the activity through the lens of a strength. If you hate confrontation, for example, but are strengthened by asking

Me & My BIG Ideas

penetrating questions, approach a potential confrontation instead as a way to ask such questions.

Take 5 minutes to reflect on the past week. Pay attention to how the tasks you did made you feel as you were doing them. Think of the SIGNs of a strength (and note that the SIGNs of a weakness are simply the reverse) and make note of activities that energized you and those that left you drained.

I felt strong (energized, engaged)...

1._____

2._____

3._____

4._____

I felt weak (drained, bored)...

1._____

2._____

3._____

4._____

Were you surprised by any of the activities that strengthened you? That weakened you? Are you finding happiness in what you are doing?

What is happiness? What does happiness mean to you?

Happiness is a mental or emotional state of well-being characterized by positive or pleasant emotions ranging from contentment to intense joy. A variety of biological, psychological, religious and philosophical approaches have striven to define happiness and identify its sources. Various research groups, including positive psychology, endeavour to apply the scientific method to answer questions about what "happiness" is and how it might be attained.

Philosophers and religious thinkers often define happiness in terms of living a good life or flourishing, rather than simply as an emotion.

Happiness can be closely associated with success!

How do you know if you're successful or happy? Do you rely heavily on objective metrics such as your job title, the size of your bank account or the colleges your children are getting into? Or do you focus more on the subjective, such as the satisfaction of solving thorny problems at work, the joy of collaborating with clever colleagues or how happy you are at home?

You might not even realize where you're placing the most emphasis until you try plotting out your success metrics in a grid.

Even if you find yourself listing mostly objective factors, the subjective elements have a way of tugging at you, don't they? The relationship between the objective and the subjective is complicated and idiosyncratic. Subjective success is an individual's response to an objective situation. A corporate lawyer may work for a highly respected firm and have a lavish compensation package, but if her career falls short of her dream to become a Supreme Court justice, for instance, or if practicing law seems merely a good way to make a living and doesn't provide an intellectual buzz, she won't feel successful, therefore she won't be happy.

Me & My BIG Ideas

Let's look at prosperity. What does prosperity entail? A lot of us believe it refers to wealth. You have all the money you need and more - more money than you can spend in a lifetime.

Prosperity is the state of flourishing, thriving, good fortune and or successful social status. Prosperity often encompasses wealth but also includes others factors which can be independent of wealth to varying degrees, such as happiness and health.

Although prosperity does include money, you don't need to have all the money in the world to feel prosperous. What you need is to be satisfied with what you do have, be grateful and firmly believe that whenever you do not have what you'd like to have it will come to you effortlessly.

Really prosperous people go through life's ups and downs in a more relaxed fashion. They have all they need and are able to manifest whatever they might need, because of a deep believe that the universe will always take care of them.

Are you satisfied? Most of us are always searching for the next best thing to make our lives better without paying attention to or being grateful for what we already have. Believe me, if you have a roof over your head, food on the table on a daily basis and clothes on your back you have a lot to be grateful for.

Having a good relationship with people is a very good way of becoming prosperous because money is attached to people and is exchanged between people and entities

Once you prosper you will start living in abundance.

"Prosper and experience complete abundance"

Me & My BIG Ideas

Become fully present in life. Being present is what we experience when we are completely at peace with this very moment. It is a life journey where we constantly grow our inner peace.

Our feelings are calm. Our reflexes are fast. Our respective minds are clear. We are decisive. We know what we want. We know what is right for us. We perform our best whether speaking in public, taking part in sports & music or relating to people. Our confidence is deep. We know and accept that we're not perfect. This lets be real. We accept we have faults and we own them.

Being present in everything that you do is the one thing that will change your life! Here are TEN practical benefits when you focus on being present:

Performance benefits:

- Better performance under pressure (you're focused)
- Improved listening and memory skills (you're "present-minded", not "absent-minded")
- Better conflict resolution (you don't get emotionally 'triggered')
- More persistence and ability to learn (you are more patient and tolerant of difficulties)
- Wiser, clearer decisions (you don't react out of habit)

Health & relationship benefits:

- Improved physical health & energy (less stress, lower blood pressure, sharper mind)
- More laughter and a playful outlook (you're at peace, so life is more joyful)
- More honest & open communication (you have nothing to hide)

Me & My BIG Ideas

- Confidence and conviction in leading others (you can handle their criticisms)
- Greater capacity for emotional intimacy (you are comfortable in your own skin)

Being in the present is a gift that lasts a life-time; the only time anything real happens is in the present moment... so "act or accept but never stay stuck!"

Chapter 8
Make it Sustainable

Deciding on a topic is very easy once you have found your passion driven talent but if not, electing a topic is difficult!

WHY?

"Because it's important"

It's right up there with choosing where to live, who to date or what degree to get. Your actions and your entire future are shaped the moment you make a decision and of course, you want it be the right one.

When someone says "the good ideas are already taken" or "there is no room left for me", what they're actually saying is this:

"I'm this close to giving up."

There are infinite amounts of ideas that can turn into sustainable businesses - even within saturated markets; you just have to spend time to figure it out. It is NOT easy; nevertheless if you really want this you cannot give up.

Selecting a topic is a long-term decision but even if it is the wrong one, it's not a long-term loss! You may fail however, as long as you learn it is time well invested. It's always good to start off on the right foot though so here are some tips and strategies to help you with your topic selection process so you can give yourself the best possible chance.

Me & My BIG Ideas

FORGET "BRAND-NEW". THINK "BETTER-NEW".

In order to succeed you cannot do what everyone else is doing.

"Follow the crowd and get lost in it"

You know this.

Unfortunately many people interpret this to mean that they have to create something totally brand-spanking new, something completely innovative in order to succeed.

This is a tall order because:

- It's difficult to think of something original.
- And if you do you are swimming in unchartered waters.

The more intelligent approach is to forget about starting fresh. Rather begin with something that is already recognized but improve it.

Be a consumer, a customer of products within that market and be conscious of your experience and the experience of others in that market as well. Read comments, reviews, participate in forums and discussions and truly get to know who your potential target audience is by becoming the target yourself. The only difference between you and everyone else in that market is that you are there on a mission to make things better.

Start by picking a market that actually interests you. The competition doesn't matter at this point – just pick something you like.

You're going to pick a sub-section within that market and then dig deeper still. Find your perfect customer, the one person that will benefit most from your solution.

Me & My BIG Ideas

A great way to get into this is by describing your ideal client - who is already a steadfast supporter? This is the first of 3 avatars…

The descriptions will be used to enable you to speak directly to these avatars in all of your marketing and sales messages as well as when you deliver your product or service. Be as specific as possible. The more detailed you are in your account of your avatars, the more effective you will be at compiling and conveying your communications. This brings us to the next part – branding!

Have you ever experienced a moment of utter frustration by the fact that you just cannot understand or remember what you are being taught? I know I have. What if there was a way for you to structure your solutions in such a way that is easy to learn, remember and teach? That is why you have to brand your solution. Brand your solution and you will have the outline of your product, your content will have structure, be easy to teach and will be easy to remember for you and your students.

You now have a topic for a product, you know who you want to sell the product to and you have an outline for your product. What's next? You need an easy content creation formula that's designed to create a steady stream of rankings, traffic and leads to any web site and business.

The content you create will:

- Cause you to be easily found online and drive traffic to your website.
- Establish credibility and trust with visitors and prospective clients.
- Distinguish you from your competitors.

Me & My BIG Ideas

- Create a demand for your product or service.
- Decrease or eliminate the need to "sell".
- Help you build a list of leads.

You'll advance your audience from not knowing anything about you to becoming qualified prospects and eventually buyers. You'll go from being a salesman to an authority, trusted advisor and friend. This is the true goal of marketing.

What you say is important but not nearly as important as how you say it and how your customers perceive it as a result. To create high-quality products that your customers will use and enjoy, you need to make sure you that you execute all three phases of product creation faultlessly: (1) structuring your content (2) producing your product (3) packaging your product for delivery.

Although you can package your product in two ways - digitally or physically, the same basic steps are required for each version. In one way or another, you need to define and showcase the following items:

- Name/Core Branding (logo, colours, overall look and feel)
- Product Title and Subtitle (the clear benefit) - this needs to be on the outside of your packaging and on every major sub-component for physical products; for online products be sure that this is on your home page and preferably each major page/section of the website.
- Social Proof/Testimonials (FTC compliant)
- Product Description (what's included) in a dominant location on outside package, cover or home page
- Copyright (put this on every piece of your packaging/page of your website)
- Trademarks notated where applicable

- Stick Letter (welcome, reinforce benefits and go over how to use the program with clear structure/steps)
- Marketing Collateral – up sells and coupons
- Phone/Email/Web Support that makes it easy for customers to get help fast

Packaging is the coordinated system of preparing goods, the technology of enclosing or protecting products for distribution, storage, sale and use. It also refers to the process of design, evaluation and production of packages. Packaging contains, protects, preserves, transports, informs and ultimately sells.

I believe you need to take your ideas and expand them, not only to create more wealth opportunities but also to help as many people as you possibly can with the solutions that you have for their problems. Your solutions could be turned into bestselling products, businesses, services or books. Would you agree that a book is so much more than a good read? Becoming an author might be one of the best, if not the best decision you could make in your life and I believe you only need to make 20 good decisions at the right time in your lifetime to become successful. What can a book do for you?

A book is about informing your readers – helping them to get to know, like and trust you… To advise your audience that you are, in fact, the authoritative expert on the problem they are hoping to solve. This book is the start of a relationship between you, like a first date – it is when and how they decide whether they want this connection. Reveal too much and you'll overwhelm them; too little and they will lose interest.

Me & My BIG Ideas

Begin with a table of contents. Upon reading the table of contents the reader ought to be able to map out the journey they'll be embarking on exactly.

How many chapters? As many chapters as is necessary to tell the story. A book is notable due to its merits, not the numbers of pages in it but tell a complete story concisely and they will value it greatly. Nonetheless in the end your audience will be impressed with your solution, not the number of pages you took to explain it.

Now write the introduction to your book, welcoming your reader and revealing the solution you are going to provide to the problem they currently have. The purpose of the introduction is to bring people deeper into what it is you do, thank them for investing in your book and outline the surprise bonuses that come with the investment. Bonuses are an indispensible tool to familiarize readers with your non-written content, like audios and videos and to help them get to know, like and trust you. If your reader finishes the introduction already thrilled with their purchase, you have won! Only after you've prepared the table of contents, the introduction, the offer and the final page, is it time to dive into writing the content.

In order to create your book you'll need nothing more than Microsoft Word or a simple and free word processor like Google Docs. Don't worry about fonts or formatting your document at first; focus on writing the text.

What is the key to writing your book? Rewrite existing content or quickly create content of your own.

"Get it down and then get it right"

It's imperative that you let a fresh pair of eyes - such as someone in your community, an assistant, or your spouse edit your content.

All editing should still be completed with no special formatting (remember what we said before about the nature of ebooks). Editing is about content, not format.

Follow these steps and you'll have a book produce worthy of a first date your audience has always dreamed of. They now know, like and trust you and you are ready for what's next.

To make your dreams and ideas sustainable takes a lot time and hard work but it is worth the blood, sweat and tears when you live the life you are meant to live, isn't it?

The next step is to create an irresistible offer.

To create an effective offer, you need to know:

- **What is their problem?** The problem has to be so clear that you could see it driving 65 miles per hour down a winding road in the rain.
- **How you will solve their problem permanently?** Why are you the only person who can solve it for them?
- **What is your proof?** What real-life examples, stories or case studies can you share as proof your product works?
- **What is your step-by-step process?** This is the system you are selling to them, the complete solution to their problem.

What goes into an offer? When creating your offer, you will need to be very clear on each of the follow ten ingredients so you can fully leverage each ingredient as it applies to you and your business. Depending on your experience and situation, you might need more or less of each ingredient. Tweak them accordingly to customize the sale. Because absolute clarity is so important, you may need to define and refine these areas several times before you arrive at your final offer. In the end, you want to make sure you have an offer that your perfect client simply can't refuse because it satisfactorily solves their problems.

YOUR IDEAL CUSTOMER & THEIR BIGGEST PAIN POINTS

In other words, you will need to know:

- Who your model customer IS. Who are your most successful, best customers?
- Who your ideal customer IS NOT. Who do you not want as your customers?
- What your customer wants and needs most.
- What is preventing them from having what they want and need most?

YOUR CREDENTIALS

Use your credentials as a positioning piece that establishes you as an expert in your field. You must establish yourself as the leading authority in your field and give your customers certainty that you are the go-to person in your area of expertise.

THE PRIMARY HOOK

If your clients could push a magic button that gives them exactly what they want, what would the button do? This is your solution and your hook.

YOUR STORY

What is your core story of transformation? How did you get to where you are today? Remember, even though this story is about your own transformation the outcome is to give your audience something they relate to and aspire to be like! In the end, it's about inspiring your potential customers vs. just telling your story.

A TRANSFORMATIONAL VEHICLE

What is the unfair advantage customers will have if they purchase your product? What challenges do most people in this market face and how are you helping them bypass this to get a fast, more certain result?

YOUR SYSTEM SOLUTION

Articulate your core system. How specifically will your product give them more of what they really want?

CORE LESSONS

What are three central lessons you can give people that will give them a taste of your solutions and leave them wanting more? This is about giving people "results in advance" - sharing a couple of tips or strategies that will make a difference for them now but doesn't give the entire solution away.

IRREFUTABLE PROOF

Who has produced the result your customers are after by using your system?

THE PRODUCT CASCADE & OFFER

Explain the specifics. What does your customer get? Tell them exactly what they're going to get, exactly what it's going to cost, how they'll receive it and what they need to do to get it.

After completing your irresistible offer by following the 9 steps above, you need to work on your speaking skills because you will deliver your irresistible offer any chance you get; business meetings, in front of small groups or even at big speaking events. This offer is your "sales pitch", do it as often as you can.

The final part of turning your passions, dreams or ideas into income and making it sustainable is to promote what you have created. You have to share your message, your products or solutions with those who need it most. Marketing has changed dramatically over the past decade, it has gone from flyers and banners to website and mobile sites, from direct mail marketing to email - and mobile marketing to social media marketing. Everything has evolved over the last couple of years, why should your marketing methods be archaic?

> "Change is inevitable, just go with it"

We are living in the information age with an extensive demand for new content, use the demand in your marketing strategy. You may want to use the following 4 marketing strategies to promote your products, services, business or yourself.

Strategy 1: Video Marketing

Video marketing is a new type of internet marketing and advertising in which businesses create short videos, 2 – 5 minutes, about specific topics using content from articles and other text sources. The videos are then uploaded to various video sharing websites like YouTube for distribution and exposure. The more videos you create and share, the more exposure you will get and thus the more sales you will generate.

There are several ways to turn articles into videos. The most traditional way is by creating a PowerPoint presentation from the original article, basically transforming the article text into an animated slideshow. Relevant pictures are then added to the slideshow and a voice-over is recorded to narrate each slide.

Finally, the presentation is recorded using screen capture software like Camtasia - the slideshow is now modified into a video that can be uploaded to a video sharing site. You don't even have to be in front of the camera if you are not comfortable with it.

Strategy 2: Email Marketing

Electronic marketing is directly marketing a commercial message to a group of people using email. In its broadest sense, every email sent to a potential or current customer could be considered email marketing. It usually involves using email to send ads, engender business or solicit sales or donations and is meant to build loyalty, trust and brand awareness. Email marketing can be forwarded to a relevant database. Generally the term is usually used to refer to:

- Sending email messages with the purpose of enhancing the relationship of a merchant with its current or previous customers, to encourage customer loyalty and create repeat business.
- Sending email messages with the purpose of acquiring new customers or convincing current customers to purchase something immediately.
- Adding advertisements to email messages sent by other companies to their customers.

"You can reach more people than what the president did in 1980, that's the power of email marketing"

Strategy 3: Mobile Marketing

Mobile marketing is marketing on or with a mobile device, such as a smart phone. Mobile marketing can provide customers with time and location sensitive, personalized information that promotes goods, services and ideas.

Marketing through cellphones' SMS (Short Message Service) became increasingly popular in the early 2000s in Europe and some parts of Asia when businesses started to collect mobile phone numbers and send off wanted (and often unwanted) content. On average, SMS messages are read within four minutes, making them highly convertible.

Over the past few years SMS marketing has become a legitimate advertising channel. This is because unlike email sent via the public internet, the carriers who police their own networks have set guidelines and best practices for the mobile media industry (including mobile advertising).

Mobile marketing via SMS has expanded rapidly. SMS has become the most popular branch of the Mobile Marketing industry with several 100 million advertising SMS's sent out every month in Europe alone.

SMS marketing services typically run off a short code, but sending text messages to an email address is another methodology (though this method is not supported by the carriers). Short codes are 5 or 6 digit numbers that have been assigned by all the mobile operators in a given country for the use of brand campaign and other consumer services.

Besides short codes, inbound SMS's can be received on long numbers (international number format, e.g. +44 7624 805000 or US number format: [5] e.g. 757 772 8555), which can be used in place of short codes or premium-rated short messages for SMS reception in several applications such as product promotions and campaigns. Long numbers are internationally available as well as enabling businesses to have their own numbers. One key criterion is that the consumer opts into the service. The mobile operators demand a double opt in from the consumer and the ability for the consumer to opt out of the service at any time by sending the word STOP via SMS.

Strategy 4: Social Media Marketing

Social media marketing refers to the process of gaining website traffic or attention through social media sites.

Social media marketing programs usually centre on efforts to create content that attracts attention and encourages readers to share it with their social networks. The resulting electronic word of mouth (eWoM) refers to any statement consumers share via the Internet (e.g., web sites, social networks, instant messages, news feeds) about an event, product, service, brand or company. When the underlying message spreads from user to user and presumably resonates because it appears to come from a trusted, third-party source, as opposed to the brand or company itself, this form of marketing results in earned media rather than paid media.

Social networking websites allow individuals to interact with one another and build relationships. When companies join the social channels, consumers can interact with them and they can communicate with consumers directly. That interaction feels more personal to users than traditional methods of strictly outbound marketing & advertising.

Me & My BIG Ideas

Social networking sites and blogs allow individual followers to "tweet" or "post" comments about the product being promoted. By repeating the message, all of the user's connections are able to see the message, therefore reaching more people. Social networking sites act as word of mouth. Because the information about the product is being put out there and is getting repeated, more traffic is brought to the product/company.

Through social networking sites, companies can interact with individual followers. This personal interaction can instil a feeling of loyalty into followers and potential customers. Also, by choosing whom to follow on these sites, products can reach a very narrow target audience.

Social networking sites also include a vast amount of information about what products and services prospective clients might be interested in. Through the use of new Semantic Analysis technologies, marketers can detect buying signals such as content shared by people and questions posted online. Understanding of buying signals can help sales people target relevant prospects and marketers run micro-targeted campaigns.

Chapter 9
The Expert Industry

3 Ways to become an Expert

An expert, generally speaking, is a person with extensive knowledge or ability based on research, experience or occupation and in a particular area of study. Doesn't that mean that there is only three ways to really become an expert? By research, report, or results! Here's 3 ways for you to enter the expert industry. Can I tell you a secret? It is not that difficult.

Let's get into this!

Becoming a Research Expert

You can research your way into the expert industry! You can become an expert on your topic by researching and reporting on your findings; the things you have learned. In your mind go back to the moment you realized what your passion is. Grab your passion, ok now you know what your topic is, let's assume you are passionate about making money, so how do you make money? Let's say you make money online meaning your topic will be "Making Money Online".

First thing you do (what most of us will do) is type into Google, making money online. You are now researching your topic. Gain as much knowledge as you can. You now have expert knowledge on making money online; all that is left to do is implement the 5 fundamentals of the expert industry which we will discuss in a moment.

Becoming a Report Expert

Becoming a report expert is by far the easiest, quickest and fastest growing way for upcoming experts. Let me ask you this; can you ask questions? Off course you can! Can you record the questions and answers? Off course you can! Then what is stopping you from interviewing that "group of people" in front of you (in your area) and report on what they had to say? All you have to do is pick up the phone, send an email or get into your car and make an appointment to interview the experts and become an expert yourself.

Become an Expert by Result

The last path to the expert industry is by showing results. To become a results expert is by far the hardest, most time consuming but the most accountable way of becoming an expert.

Saying you are an expert in making money online and having the figures to prove it automatically makes you the go to person in your field.

The 5 foundations of wealth

Why do you want to be seen as an expert? We have now ascertained that there are 3 ways for you to become an expert. Whether you want to make more money, grow your business, spend more time with your family or help other people - whatever it is that you want to do; you need to implement your expertise into the 5 foundations of wealth. The 5 foundations of wealth are what will make you money in this industry. Sticking to our example of making money online, you have now reached expert status by either researching; reporting or you have results to show. Now you are going to implement the 5 foundations of wealth. You don't have to apply all 5 foundations but I strongly recommend that you practice as many of them as you possibly can because each foundation of wealth is a possible income stream.

Foundation 1: Writing

The first foundation of wealth is writing. I'm not saying you have to be the next William Shakespeare. Your main objective is to get your potential customers to know, like and trust you, your book should build credibility, not make you millions at least not just yet.

Writing a book for credibility - isn't that just too much work to get people to know and trust you? Not whatsoever, you have done your research or interviewed some experts, you already have the content for your book, all you have to do is put it together and get it edited. Visit www.theauthormaker.co.za, this is the technology you need to get your book sold with mobile optimized lead capture and sales pages with automated follow up email and text campaigns. You can start selling your book in less than a week. Isn't this way better than the conventional way of book marketing? How would it impact you and your business if your book was listed next to the books of your heroes? What would that mean for your lifestyle?

Foundation 2: Speaking

Foundation 2 is all about speaking, teaching and building your list of potential future customers while making a profit doing it. Public speaking is the process and act of speaking or giving a lecture to a group of people in a structured, deliberate manner intended to inform, influence or entertain a listening audience. It is the face-to-face conversation between individuals and an audience for the purpose of communication, closely allied to "presenting", although the latter is more often associated with commercial activity. Most of the time, public speaking is to persuade the audience.

You have to persuade audiences (preferably your target market) that you have the solution to their problems - the same audience that you add to your database for future events or offers with the crowd maker. How on earth can you add 70% of your audience to your list at once? That is what the crowd maker is all about. The campaign captures leads anywhere, anytime! This campaign utilizes multiple channels for your prospect to subscribe to, this way you can offer a method that people are familiar with.

The ease with which you can launch your crowd maker makes it ideal to use for all of your promotion events like:

- Trade shows
- Meetups
- Referrals
- Advertisements
- Business cards
- Teleseminars
- Webinars
- Licecasts
- Group Presentations
- Literally Anywhere

The crowd maker was designed to fit your respective needs and occasions while you watch the leads pour in.

The campaign includes:

- Multi-channel lead capture flyer

 -SMS (long code and short code)

 -QR code

 - Website URL

- Mobile optimized lead capture website

- Follow-up auto responders

Get the Crowd maker and watch your list grow rapidly, visit www.thecrowdmaker.co.za

Foundation 3: Seminars

A seminar is a form of academic instruction, either at an academic institution or as offered by a commercial or professional organization. It has the function of bringing together small groups for recurring meetings, focusing each time on some particular subject in which everyone present is requested to actively participate. This is often accomplished through an on-going Socratic dialogue with a seminar leader or instructor, or through a more formal presentation of research. Normally, participants are not beginners in the field under discussion. This is what experts do - teaching your subject, getting paid to do it, capturing more leads and offering your solutions to the people who need it. It's a win-win situation.

Now there are some things that need to be done in order for you to have a successful seminar. You have to fill up the room, have your offer presentation ready and capture leads at such an event.

You know now that you can capture at least 70% of your audience with the crowd maker but you can also have an event selling machine in place. This operation gives you an online sales page where you can receive payments for your events, get an automatic follow-up and reminders of your event delivered and then have the details added to your buyers list. You can get all this in place within a couple of days. Get your event selling machine on www.theeventmaker.co.za

"Fill up your seminars; it's the right thing to do"

Foundation 4: Coaching

Have you ever heard of passive income? Passive income is an income received on a regular basis, with little effort required to maintain it. When you make sales without being present, you are generating passive income. Coaching someone however necessitates your presence but not if you record the coaching sessions and sell it as products online. You can coach millions of people while you are on some exotic island, focusing your attention on your next important project or spending time with your loved ones. That is the power of the 5 foundations of wealth. You can make a lot of money and it is automated! You can make money while you sleep!

How do I sell my coaching programs on line? The product maker - it is a simple one-page sales machine that makes processing payments and selling online easier than ever before. This machine allows you to set up your page without worrying about any of the security, programming or hosting requirements. I

The Product Maker includes a sales squeeze page, a thank you confirmation page, and finally your membership delivery page.

A single welcome/confirmation auto responder will give your members their access link. If you are already coaching or will be coaching in the future, you have to see the product maker in action. Visit www.theproductmaker.co.za Start selling your products online and create another income stream.

Foundation 5: Online Marketing

Marketing is one of the most important factors when it comes to the business of making money as you may well know. The 5th foundation of wealth is online marketing. If you don't market your product or services, you will not be known by the people who need your products or services most. Info Products(PTY) Ltd.'s strategies has been proven to work in almost any line of business helping multiple entrepreneurs, authors, speakers, coaches, consultants, small business owners and individuals get discovered in the online world and is now available to you. Some of our strategies include:

The Promotion Maker

The Promotion maker helps you promote your content and build your client list through multiple channels. It is centred on a single flyer page that works as a crowd capture campaign giving people multiple opportunities to opt-in to your list and then it follows up and communicates with them several times through a special, automated campaign. In other words, it's a single sheet of paper that you keep with you wherever you go. The audience sign up for a free bonus and thereby supplies you their contact information. It includes an opt-in flyer, a lead page and a thank you/confirmation page.

Promote your business, products or services with the promotion maker, visit www.thepromotionmaker.co.za

The Expert Maker

The Expert Maker will create a video blog site that consists of 4 pages. Use this machine to create the content for these pages, it's quick and easy.

- ✓ Get people to know, like and trust you.
- ✓ Instantly position yourself as the recognized expert and authority in your field.
- ✓ Create your expert site to establish credibility and help you get found online as well as your video blog for your book, product or service.

Visit www.theexpertmaker.co.za to enter the expert industry today.

Me & My BIG Ideas

Please visit us at ExpertIndustry.co.za for your free product creation guide and expert industry presentation video on discovering the possibilities the industry hold for small business owners, big corporations, entrepreneurs, authors, experts, speakers, coaches and consultants

We'll share our best, cutting-edge strategies for creating your own product from scratch, or maximizing a product you already have, but that may not be producing the income or impact you desire.

Info Products (PTY) Ltd

17 Mimosa Street, Wilropark

Johannesburg, SA 1731

+2711 025 5462

www.expertindustry.co.za

www.ingramcontent.com/pod-product-compliance
Lightning Source LLC
Chambersburg PA
CBHW072040190526
45165CB00018B/1292